❖

From a Balcony in Palos Verdes

from a BALCONY
in PALOS VERDES

SEAN MCGRATH

wor(l)ds publishing
Los Angeles

wor(l)ds publishing
Los Angeles, California

Paperback ISBN 978-0-578-28713-3 (First Edition)

Cover Photo by Kenneth Cowan
Cover Design by Jamie Kennedy and Wendy L. D. Staples
Interior Layout by Sean McGrath
Printed in Los Angeles by Indie Printing

For musical accompaniment follow the "Joyous Balcony" playlist
by seanermc17 on Spotify.

for my neighbors

The world's rumor stirred in forests,
later the wheat blazed, pixilated
with flowers red as burns,
then autumn arrived to introduce
the scripture of wine:
it all passed, the fugitive sky
was summer's out-held glass,
and the junketing cloud burned off.

—*Pablo Neruda*

CONTENTS

<u>Frequencies</u>

❖

From a Balcony in Palos Verdes

1

Front Balcony at Dusk

        a brewing storm
on the left coast
             of my heart

                steady breeze on the right

and in the center
        the very tiny
            pinpoint center
the cool inescapable truth
        of human design

—man, what a party

Turning In

planes
  planes and trains
    and plains

stretching endlesslessy
  rounding ceaselessly

in a world that never rests
  rest is the only respite

it's why i nap everyday!

  facing skyways
    feet untucked

my team upon me like a weighted blanket—
  pillows with heartbeats
    —they dictate the rhythm of my dreaming

my mind's eye is altogether different
  than the poet's eye
    life is often violent
      full of crashing and confusion

i wake to the thunder of a plane
　sailing through my very room
　　where there was no plain at all
　　　or sound

but out here
　on this balcony
　　in especially cool breezes
　i can turn my head just a little
sideways
　　listen in
　　　instead of out
　and see those other things
　deep in my dreams
　　that the waking world
　　would have me forget

San Pedro Sonder

thursday
  eight a.m.
steam lifts from the track
  doing laps for the great race
of morning
last night's rainfall vaporing off
under a late-winter sun—

  it is just we out there
  two dogs and I who
walk out to the edge and gaze upon
the docks of San Pedro

  the beauty is not lost on me
there should be a rainbow somewhere!
  maybe there is
    here in my heart

some days are like this you know—
  you wake with a love for all people
  and all things
  and you can't quite tell why

From a Balcony in Palos Verdes

"There is a moving palace that floats in the air
with balconies and clear water flowing through,
infinity everywhere, yet contained under a single tent." –Rumi

Beyond the whiteness
of day, before the solitude of night,
a hue to better suit my mood:
333 m track orange, towers clustered in gold,
eyes of city lights at sundown, freedom
in the falling leaves,
pomes burst from the toyon...

The color of a pulsing beat,
music, jazz is alive at the fingertips,
the time for gnashing teeth is far off

... I see a world of restless blinks
blinking in recycled air, and beyond:
a flash storing up the backsides of mountains

—the flood we all dream in—

Come fill this gas-tank-heart,
s(t)eal wor(l)ds in me whose passcode
is this very hue now faded.

"What Kind of Times Are These"
after Adrienne Rich

There's a place on the hill where
three pines and a sycamore grow at
right angles from each other:

at night they form a diamond and at dawn
they make a cross and at day
you'd hardly notice unless you knew.

I've sat between them in the twilight
and I've watched the mountain sun clamber
through their limbs in summer, bringing their color
and sometimes stealing away the dew of morning.

I've seen strips of bark drop from the sycamore with a sound
and pine dust fill the drive on Santa Ana days
and I've heard creatures of the undergrowth talk
about the burning of the hill—but don't be fooled
this is not a fiery poem, there is enough around
to tell us of the end now.

And I won't tell you where this place is, nor the angle
you need to see how the trees have formed like this
on purpose—I know already people who want to raze them,

level it, and build on the nothing left behind.

And I won't tell you where it is, so why do I tell you anything?
Because you still listen, because in times like these
to have you listen at all, it's necessary to talk about trees.

We've Lost the Trail

"Each breaking wave, each rush of the sea on the slope of sand, reminds me why these places of pilgrimage matter. They matter to me because in the long view, I do not. I am driftwood. I am rockweed. I am osprey and the mackerel in the clutch of her feet. I am a woman standing on the edge of the continent looking out." –Terry Tempest Williams

Tell them it happened this time on the
Ishibashi Trail, Palos Verdes
And that they won't need to come for me
anymore
The bend (in me) has gone gray and green
and back again

I can see the change in blues of the old
flat pacific from here
And the southern islands cloud-smothered
miles off

Tell them the invaders could use a little rain
but can't they always
Though, truthfully, their uniform dry stalks
swaying tall, crackling, is handsome, if not troubling

We are reminded, there are some
places where houses should not be built—

the ground just won't break

See the moles dart in and out across us,
dog and I, and too many lizards to count
We've gone in so deep we've forgotten
there could be men around

When he growls I sing back, laughing
a sort of bird call
He picks up scents like on a river raft
nose pulling him as gravity does
down to the sea

Tell them I have been running, fixing these trails
and they can meet me at the final dusk
when the long sun has come down at last

We might be out wading in the salt
or we may be here, atop the western hills, the
verdant bluffs, sage-lined trails,
with the scent of buckwheat everywhere
and a song in my heart called Pilgrim

Tell them
we might just stay here a while,
until the shadow of the tree has lipped the night

the fire inside still brimming
the land a spark away

❖

fighting hummingbirds (hearts aflutter)
  they are three then one and then three again
    as us
   who come separate and leave nearly so
    if perhaps a drop heavier
     some otherment what clung to us
      in that wet mad tangle
   such a blur you'd hardly know it
    but for the lookers
     who chanc'd upon it
      on their wingéd exit

Nestling

They say the coos of the lone mourning dove
are filled with grieving

So this morning I wake to her familiar
call, of backyards and old losses.

In the burning sun, she picks dead
pines from the undergrowth,

Flaps them heavy up to the nook where—
look at that, it was not she-dove

But he, carrying the floor to mother,
who sits warm on hoping things.

They say the mourning dove pairs for life,
and songs of grieving carry high notes too.

Songs From Isolation

1

a grand piano sings for the freeway on the slowest day
man plays furiously as if to say—some stay in the breakdown
lane and leave there their lives the man plays a low note high
and the black key flies upupup beyond the fading sky
he plays into night and kids they say ma i've never seen
a day so long i've never heard a song so bright

4

Goodman licks a trail on the balcony floor
    each lash of the tongue a footprint
  in the pollen of time
    each stroke in this book a landmark
  to guide me (back) home

6

I found you!
    little hummer
  nesting upon this piney branchlet
the sap is your seat
   the needles your blinds
  and eons of instinct
   the recipe to understanding
  how to hold up
    in a wind

11 (going outside)

baby kitten
weighing nothing
climbs up the screen

young cat
weighing some
leaps and holds on

full grown
she slides it open
with her sweet cat nose

17

in this sun hour even the dead
pine needles take on a red hue
—no, golden—a cool, blowy
day, and I think:
this is what forgiveness can do
to a man

18

all the trees were tipped the same way
and I wondered if the inland breeze
made them like so, softly tiltworn
after so many seasons, but then I
picked my head off the railing
blinked open my other eye and realized
hey! I still got half a beer here

22

an excellent soreness in my legs upon waking;
the seven a.m. sun well through its cover,
rabbit in the brush, peafowl calls in
the air, hatchlings in the sycamore—
there is no cloning them:
these new days just keep coming, one at a time

28

she nuzzle-noses this page and that
  then puts a cheek to my pen for scritches
but I don't lift it
  and she don't mind
  write on   little us   write on

Yield for Horses

for the locals

There be ranchers here, horsemen
And lady riders
Who rise before light, set the bit
And take to the bridle trails:
Browndeer, Seahurst, Santa Bella—
Do you know them? Do you hear
The hoofclops amid the warming day?

Some of us do; others we wake
With the rooster, with the crowing peacock,
With the sun which rolls in over the Gabriel
Range like a long white wave—

Where is this place, where the horsemen clop
And the ranges stand stark in the summer light?
Where you can go from sea to sycamore to
Mountain passes all before the break of noon—
Where the eucalypts shed their menthy bark and
Lizards hide from hawks in the underwood—
Where the jacarandas purple-petal the lawns
And the pines shower whole hoods in their yellow-violent
Sneezy stamens of life?

Of green sticks, where the seafarer roams,
Of bikers and runners moving two abreast
Up the hill where the lone brown cat sits
Bathing in hot light,
Of the hilltop, where three fluffy dogs wait
In the window to bark at the night,
Of tidepools and jagged cliffsides
Where the vines forever grow,
Of the ranchland, where they brought water
On their backs until this hard-pack broke blossom
And settlers broke pacts with the earth
To watch for the waiting fire—

Where poets live, brimming with scribbly, inky rhythm,
Trying to pull back the past:
Indigenous Dawn, two quarreling deities,
and a pure white eagle captaining the land—
Do you know them? Do you hear their gentle
Gentle, heavy-heavy plodding hoofclops
Upon this paper lane?

2

whose echoes carry generations

all of this thunder and crashing
  the world brinking
like some swollen titan
  has kicked it off its axis
    fire   gunships
  exploding planes
a forest of gallows on the seashore
  waiting for nighttime

I have so many fears
she tells me
  but only because I have so much
left to live!

  there is always god,
I would say   but maybe not
  this I know:
    these words
      this binding
this black and white
  in the turbulent night
  like an arm of stone
defends me

and me too?

come to my chest, hear the drumming
whose echoes carry generations back and forth
  hear it
    there is no place it cannot find you

Sunday Morning Acoustic

laid up in bed
with coffee and a big cozy
we invite the dogs back in
who reclaim their nooks and nuzzle
between us, love, hearts beating
still and the blinds full drawn,
with no rush at all
to get at the day

Crossword Spring

a bug sets
  then a thousand
    and before you know it
    they've up and flown off
with your bookcase

  kids tagging trees
with sidewalk chalk look up
  and see the floating library

gone with the wind drops down
    clunks little fathead straight on
    his temple wells up plum size
      out comes mom cursin the heavens

but they've moved on
  cross the valley an' over
    the toy mountain
      leavin bread crumb paperbacks
    stretched cross the city
      til the words make news and

drunk meteorologist says bring an umbrella
  the flies are out and they're shitten in our eyes

but gramma knows best, remembers,
  stick your tongue out when it happens

t a s t e
    the man made
        s
          k
            y

she skates along a line in the air

Rolling reds
        wind like waves

3-dog balcony
        and a 2-D sky

Here's a metaphor:
cat tiptoes on the ledge looking out at old mountains—
        will she jump?

An oak leaf grabs a current of air
freewhirls up thirty good feet and sticks on a tree branch:
        someone is playing the world in reverse

(if all things have a zenith
        then when does the day peak?)

When the cat does jump
        a story above ground
I can feel the moment gravity slips out of socket
        like an earthquake from the clouds

There is no fall—she skates along a line in the air
        for a whole exhale

Before stepping back to the ledge
    she never left.

Snake Out Back

A snake lives there.
Go see,
he is tied to the water hose
and can't get within two feet of the house,
which is too bad—he's starving.

You kids think he looks friendly,
think starving's no fun,
welp, there he goes
eating all the cat food
and worse he's got a whole basketball hoop
wrapped around his neck. See,
look at him
tearing up the lawn.

The dog's pregnant too,
yup,
that's what all that sneezing was about
and now they're out:
six of them,
size of mice and colorful—
they pee the wood floors.
Grandpa calls a plumber to fix a leak
he don't know.

And now what?

The cat's gone out there to get her food back,

we know how this goes

senseless meddling I told you—

great,

they're playing basketball together,

they'll probably get drafted.

You know, you could've just let it suffer.

"Allowables"

after Nikki Giovanni

it rains in the morning
  and the children they race
inside and under big tents
  they are underdressed
and you can tell how young they are
  by how they refuse to shiver

we return to the key of our piece:
  is there other evidence that allows us
  to read race into Giovanni's poem?
  the spider as brown recluse
  the other a black widow!

it could also... just be
about spiders? one boy
with cold-nipped knees asks—
you can tell how young they are
  by how they refuse to shiver

3

9/14

a september of smoke
and i kid you not
the spiders were crawling on the sky

their silken lines hung down from nowhere
barely distinguishable in this ashen scape

a plane found out the hard way
caught its wing in a web
and went hurtling 180 back across the sea

there weren't passengers in it anyway—
the last two were beheaded for coughing and now
the planes just did their routes in the stealthy cover

of wildfire so they could dump things into the water:
plastics and bones and film reels and things they
could no longer fit in the museums—

if a culture falls in the ocean and nobody hears it,
will it wash up on a third-world island ten years later?

the crows caw double in all this burning
the babies cough triple and us?

we have drinks the color of puddles as

the civic center is airlifted into a spinny tomb the
freeways sprout tiny freeways to nowhere is anybody seeing this
there's a thousand cars and counting

piled up on top of skid row and i know
for a fact there was a tree here yesterday
don't try and convince me otherwise—

i have no doubt
about the spiders, kids,
go out and have a look yourselves,

it's amazing the things they'll do when
they think no one is watching

9/20

still here
  on this balcony
as the smoke blots out the sun
as the day turns red
as the moon turns to ash
  the rain is ash
  the night is ash
the dog brings me a small poop in her mouth
   it is ash

the ends of summer
like a campsite in mourning—
i won't make much more of it
  we know the drill
    we hurtle on and on into a bigger disaster
small fires lighting the sullen path
 starved lunatics licking rust from the undercarriage

this poem is the shape of a city
this poem is the shape of a city

9/21: The World Spins Madly On

the dead were in the wind—
four hundred thousand cremations and counting
as the santa anas poured inout the starstruck valley
I, sitting on the balcony as the pines broke,
sucking in whorlds of this
  curious smoke
    like nothing i've tasted
      since

drones, mechanical fliers millions
chasing rats down the alleys
crashing windways into loud things;
 a building lopped open
in one clean slice, its innards
papaya flesh, screaming
men in suits jumping out like seeds
into the electric river
  power—power everywhere
unharnessed and buzzing in the
  smoking darkness the lights
   of the street exploding neon
lava onto billboards
   a gooping swarm of roaches
emerge from the ad and take to the air

I follow their trail
out above the treetops
  across a horse dung pasture
 and into the sunken airport
here is the host scene:
the tarmac is melting
a black ooze drinks towards
the great steamhouse

wind the when rushies in
we catch a clear sight of
it before the smoke dreams again:
  the furnace
burning with the engines of
a hundred jets screaming
  and bodies
   bodies like luggage [language?]
failling from the revolutionary staircase
  down to the tarry pit,
tanker after landing tanker lined up
  to shove their load
   down to earth
    into air

some crafts carry no covers,

some luggage is unzipped
some bodies
    not quite frozen bodies
  lurch around before the big quake
   the electronic scanner
tears apart two sticky waists, sniffs the
 entrail
    confirms they're dead
before they pull the lever
and the smoke blows again

but those eyes,
  those eyes I recognize
   I've seen this before,
  the wind howls
 into the void

9/22: Equinox
or, **Who is the Happy Warrior**

It was not so bad
  this pain that looked like
    the end of all things

This scorched sky
  the oily seas
    the parched earth
      and the gunshot moon

This incurable affliction
  to feed and feed
    and fuck things fast
      to rope the earth
        til we breathe our last

It was not so bad
  this feverish form today
    the splitting in my chest
      the bloodred eyes and
        hands without caress

For the days turn cooler
  the seas' diamond glimmer renews

the earth flips over
and the moon heals too

We treat ourselves with poetry
with music and sweat and hallowed things
we break the bread amid the storm
and bare our souls unto the eve

The light comes back into your eyes
you hear the trumpets reign again
the neighbors emerge for sunset
and place you in your zen:
writing here upon the stage
as the season now begins

10/5

shivery cold with the sailing wind
trying to lift a mighty despair off his chest
he sang out at tidebreak:
"I thought I would find you here!"
his knees, dumb with sacrifice, ached in the sand

quietly they spoke back to him
in a language he could not yet comprehend

High Tide

tehe
we drank
we smoked
we watched the water come in
one big gulp at a time

what those around us were losing
in sweat and weight
we gained in laughter

—the silliness that comes
at the edge of the land
looking out
having forgotten the meaning
of the word infinitesimal

Redondo Illusion

A kite fighting sharp in the sky,
long green tail and curves like a preybird;

I know it is a kite because,
well, I know.

But for the toddler—who has not been trained
to see fiberglass lines against the Redondo sun,

whose eyes are fixed skyward as it dips and draws,
and who cannot see the man a dune away, pulling the strings

—who reaches clenched fists to grab at it,
the illusion is perfect.

10/11

  monday
    open blue
 from here to Malibu
the whole southland
just splendid with it

72 and not even a jetstream in the sky

only the half moon
  suspended there like the conductor
   of these tides

of course the world was burning
but down here
       on this sandy level
even the kid poking at a washed up gull
  couldn't tell

At the Sandy Theatre

they gather on the shore by the hundreds
facing the same way: seaward, west,
drying off in the wind, awfully quiet,
as if waiting for the movie dusk to begin

10/21: At Sea, After Light

The marine wall poured onto the coastline
   this evening's moving mountains—
went the sailboats, went the doves,
   lines of sunset streaked through
like tunnel paths for the seagone.
   More boats, droves of pelican and cranes
fleeting from sight, making their winged exit;
   the air was wet with longing.

I shivered on the shore
   underdressed, ill-equipped to harness
all the heaven before me,
   so much of it leaking out,
coming in at once.

I can't have a cold room when it knocks—
   I should have fire in my lungs
and only a little fear in my heart,
   I should learn to warm myself
amid the wavery sea,
   to be still in the absence of light.

Yellow Eyes

the frost lines in the newnight sky
  remind me to tell you
    how cold it is on the moon:

the bolded moon drifting
  on a skyraft
   aglow and
  shinnying somewhere south
 in the flipped Atlantic—

it's warmer there they say
  but cold all around this week

     ...an atmospheric river...

is that the chill I feel walking the field
at pitch black spotting a canine
who has spotted me first?

I've seen you before you know
if only in dreams
your heart is a pulse on the wind
your bones are pure night
you sneak through the back gate

leaving only your eyes behind

yellow eyes

two dots on the skyraft
    what was such a majestic beast doing in this light?
  I said to myself
floating now some way starboard
skinny and clever again
    aching for a good hunt
  and thinking of gold things long ago unearthed
      using the forever map
    to take me back to land

11/1: For Carbon Canyon

Thick twilight mist
covers the city
quieting the air

I remember a redwood grove
in Orange County
where an old coyote lived alone

She'd come out in these hours
watching the above
weep with moist
onto the needles

Don't be sad
she said to the runner
it is how the trees drink

Listen quietly now
in the soft night
they are humming
hear them grow

Kicking Around

a night so clear
that if you turned your head quickly
you might mistake the ribbons of jetstream
for a streak of pure white lightning
in the blankety blue

a night so clear you could taste
the mountains in your lungs

we ran for hours
chasing yellow balls and soccer balls
laughing and saying how we thought it would
be much colder for this time of year

looking out on the city towers
until the glow of sunset came down on them
they sparkled golden pink red then orange—
til we knew the holiday was here

... Like Fire Unbound

The foam atop a hazy beer,
mist drawing in from the sea,
  the life of cricket, songbird,
owls, peafowl, a coyote creeps;
  the love of the valley
and the pop of color
  coming out from the green—

life again, life, over and over,
  this dusk, this season,
this year this covid year,
  this life, my life.

Like a matchstick,
  like stored energy going red,
like the flame like life:
  We are contagious, hot, free,
wanting more peace,
  craving the dark to light,
and a good soul
  to burn with.

  In wandering the
desert, I come upon a wall,

soft detritus stacked elegantly,
stacked by a nameless artist,
  it blinks in my mind
without cost:

  did you know
those who mined the sky
fell through it?
  The desert is a waitpost
for the skylorn.

  I dream of bridges
that rise skyward
  with no guardian rail
or traffic markings to take me forth,
  and I do not drive well
in my sleep.

  I dream of friends coming late
to brunch with their music blaring
  having gotten no sleep,
and ordering a round for the elders,
  who laugh and laugh in symphony.

I dream of toast,
I dream of the shadow hand of god

giving birth to things in the pacific,
the sand asks questions,
the spawning shells ask questions
the gull the motorboat
the shimmery wake all across
the sunlit southland—
there is no need to fear
the answers, no time
to doubt the heart,
what is strong shall be strong,
what is gone shan't be long:

the things we love in the world
(music, rest, poetry and loss)
have their ways of returning to us
time and time again.

Find me on a rainbow blanket
  somewhere between here and the sea
full of ink and happiness
  and a dumb drooling look in my mouth
to disguise my age;

find me on an unmarked trail
  using my feet to guide me
riverlike down to the confluence;

find me at the rubble of walls,
in a scrap of broken chains,
  in a field of abandoned nests
writing songs about fire and freedom,
  grabbing notes from the crying wind
to blurry all the meaning;

find me planting flowers in the wet cracks
of chaos settled—
  somewhere between nowhere and the sky.

$$\underline{4}$$

River Feet

This time it is a river you are
and in which you are aloft
crashing down the canyon walls
on a rainy holiday eve
tarrying with you pieces that are not
quite timebound
a great ride
to the sea

But unlike the fresh water
when you meet her tides
and all life swirls anew before you
in the confluence
it is not in you to bear out into the big
wet next step

You must turn back
and many times over
take the climb back up
on foot

Sky, Clear as Water

the evenstorm gives way
to Christmas day
and the miracle sun blasts
clarity upon the whole valley
into the newsnowed mounts
up the cloudless blue
and beyond

the planes over the city
float about in slow motion
the Hollywood sign is a short white line
on the hilltop
and closer still
a red-tail hawk sits on a pine perch
belting out its trinity call
to all us small rustlers down below—
who designed this smokeless day? is this holy?

Riddles from the Trail

with lines from Pablo Neruda

I hit the trail with speed—
       it's like this:

      I hop me hop stone to stone
  til all the good stones are unstoned

      the rabbit jump in, back out,
propagate the brush a dozen

     nine, seven
every other prime is a number here
  where these feet pound dust
   outpace the riddle wax in
my mind shoosh the wind blews
  my hoofbeats count heart
     the time

I smell the rain a season early
  bring the weather back west with me

I watch my cat become a dog

my dogs come cat-like and my
succulents shine in the dew mist
  shivering with ecstasy for rain

Winter Garden—depression and madness
  are the grasping hands of heat,
    here comes the cool
      fog sweep like over the shorn valley
  a hundred balconies n counting
      the haze billows off
    to the nethers
      the marine clouds
  are toxins taking off from our wet lungs
        old sadness outprocess
    I come again renewed

  try kneeling
try submission
  try to track one star
for six straight nights
  on the seventh   it'll come to you

Winter Garden—the blinkling sky is
eternity's outstretched hand

long road back there
    know this:
when the starfire burns out
    it is not heat annihilated
it is life spread over and past
    what light can write

the rumor of the moon
    crept in we slivered it clean
chotchkied like hangmen
    to our tether necks
    seen it ever?
kiddy diddle slip away

    now things begin to make clear:
you wait for sight of the mountains
    and want for drip of the snow
when the wheat stops blazing
    you'll be a man no more

the earth is a shingle on the
    crooked wing of a ship
blasted incandescent
    having just another big

turn
  with the while of us
glued to our blankets
  shaky cold and hinging
gum in our pockets
  and teeth ten thousand years too old for all this

  shiver not
read-y fellows
  de billow so still n right
restless county take care on you
  marny tilt wit trite

to be read under a night sky

after Babak Tafreshi

the incredible
dynamic range
of the human eye
detecting the
very faint
and the very bright
at once:

tendrils of smoke from the incense
the constellations
the lunar disk
the glint in yours
as you read this
on a cool
dark eve

The Tradition

As far back as we know
   there have been words in the air
and hands trying to fix them concrete:
       hieroglyph, papyrus, tattoo,
        oracle bone,
          blood on something unbloody,
the ink pours relentless,
   there is no dam in eternity
     to stop it.

You join here, the tradition,
   under stars by candlelight,
    with wind and trees and drink
   and passportaling open at the close of an eye—
the bluffs of albion,
   a campfire on the rim of savannah,
    the dreary cold seaboats what once bore you aloft—
your soul's asunder now,
   ease into the wonderment,
    the pen draws out the ever-ancient:
feathers the size of a cannon,
   jewelry lit around a dancer's neck,
    storms, storms of haste battering the rockbare plain;
  wrestle about til skin and blood and earth make its best color

by the moonlight.

Your body is a dream
        stuck upon a screen in the wind
              looking in, out,
                    empty and floating to a billion places
at once
        the underbrush salutes your verve,
        howls echo endless backforth in the newcarve canyon.

I am dust.
I am water.
I am ink.
I am a gun that can't kill.
I am a horn blows,
a door slams,
a dog barks in the stillness evading;
the now comes back to you   for now
but you've been found
on this
circle blue,
join us
you who are you.

Frequencies

23	like	23
21	all	21
20	back	20
18	here	18
15	things	15
14	know	14
14	wind	14
13	tell	13
13	now	13
12	down	12
12	sky	12
11	when	11
11	life	11
10	just	10
10	see	10
10	some	10
10	night	10
10	how	10

These poems were written between 2018 and 2021 in Southern California.

The epigraph for the title poem "From a Balcony in Palos Verdes" is from Jalal al-Din Rumi's "Moving Water."

The final stanza and the structure for "What Kind of Times Are These" are from Adrienne Rich's poem of the same name.

The epigraph for "We've Lost the Trail" appears in Terry Tempest William's *The Hour of Land: A Personal Topography of America's National Parks* and Maria Popova's article for The Marginalian.

"Yield For Horses" recalls the Tongva peoples as the ancestral caretakers of Tovaangar — the modern California Southland from Palos Verdes to San Bernardino, including the L.A. basin and Channel Islands, and parts of Orange County. Indigenous stories are often invisible to residents, or they are flattened as relics of the past. The poem strives to acknowledge their presence before the violent arrival of colonial settlers and now among our urban landscape.

"Allowables" was inspired by Nikki Giovanni's poem of the same name.

Several lines in "Riddles from the Trail" also appear in Pablo Neruda's poem "Winter Garden."

Several lines in "to be read under a night sky" are by Babak Tafreshi, from *The World at Night*.

The epigraph for this book is by Pablo Neruda, from "Winter Garden," translated by Forrest Gander in *The Essential Neruda: selected poems*.

I would like to thank Evan J. Coleman, Jamie Kennedy, and Aminah Aliu for their help in editing at various stages during my writing process, and Jon Okafor for his help in the production process.

I would like to thank Chadwick School in Palos Verdes for support and residence during the completion of this book.

And anyone who has ever stayed up reading with me into the late hours, thank you too.

About the Author

Sean McGrath is a poet and educator who has resided in the Northeast and the Southwest of the United States. His work has appeared in publications throughout the U.S. and his first collection, *Oculus*, was released in 2016.

Inquiries can be made to him at sean.mcgrath.writes@gmail.com.